FAMOUS
CRYPTOGRAPHERS

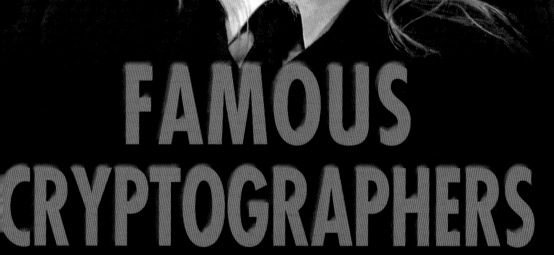

FAMOUS CRYPTOGRAPHERS

JERI FREEDMAN

ROSEN
PUBLISHING®

New York

Published in 2017 by The Rosen Publishing Group, Inc.
29 East 21st Street, New York, NY 10010

Copyright © 2017 by The Rosen Publishing Group, Inc.

First Edition

Library of Congress Cataloging-in-Publication Data

Names: Freedman, Jeri, author.
Title: Famous cryptographers / Jeri Freedman.
Description: First edition. | New York: Rosen Publishing, 2017. | Series:
Cryptography: code making and code breaking | Includes bibliographical references and index.
Identifiers: LCCN 2016017424 | ISBN 9781508173120 (library bound)
Subjects: LCSH: Cryptographers—Biography—Juvenile literature. | Cryptography—History—Juvenile
literature. | Ciphers—History—Juvenile literature.
Classification: LCC Z103.3 .F74 2017 | DDC 652/.80922 [B]—dc23
LC record available at https://lccn.loc.gov/2016017424

Manufactured in China

CONTENTS

INTRODUCTION

Cryptography is the study of secret writing. The word comes from the Greek *kryptos* (hidden) and *graphia* (writing). Cryptography includes the creation of codes and ciphers, and the decryption, or decoding, of secret messages. Keeping political, military, and diplomatic information confidential has always been a matter of utmost importance. Royalty, diplomats, generals, spies, and criminals have all relied on codes and ciphers to keep their secrets. Their enemies and rivals have pursued ways to break those codes with equal enthusiasm.

Political intrigue, secret plots, warfare, and financial gain have been part of every society throughout history. Wherever secrets need to be kept, cryptography flourishes. As far back as 1900 BCE, the ancient Egyptian scribes created special hieroglyphs to mystify and amuse their clients. Archeologists have found ancient Mesopotamian clay tablets, dating from 1500 BCE, that were clearly intended to disguise the meaning of their text. Examples of simple ciphers used by Hebrew scholars have been found that date from 600 to 500 BCE.

In the earliest forms of cryptography, correspondents manipulated the letters and words of communications written by hand. As technology advanced, so did the means of performing encryption and decryption. Mechanical devices were built that used rotating cylinders to randomly replace the letters in a word. When computer technology was developed, it became possible to generate more complex forms of encryption and to decipher encrypted documents with incredible speed.

ADAHOONIŁIGII

THE NAVAHO LANGUAGE MONTHLY

VOL. 2 NO. 3   WINDOW ROCK, ARIZONA   JANUARY 1, 1947

'AHKEAH HONEESNÁ 'ÁKO BÉÉSH BĄĄH DAH NAAZ NILÍGÍÍ YÁ DAH NÁNÍDAAHÍ SILĮĮʼ!!

Niłch'its'ósí ńdizídę́ę́ bighi' Naabeehó binant'a'í béésh bąąh dah naaznilígíí yá dah nánídaahii dooleeł biniighé Sam 'Ahkeah dóó Chéé Dodge diné naaltsoos bá 'adayiiznil. Sam 'Ahkeah naaltsoos díįdi miil dóó ba'aan naakidi neeznádiin bá 'aníídee'. Chee Dodge t'éiyá naaltsoos naakidi miil dóó ba'aan naakidi neeznádiin bá 'aníídee'.

Sam Ahkeah k'ad naanishtsoh haa deet'á, 'éí hoł bééhózin. Sam Ahkeah t'éiyá Naat'áanii Néézdę́ę́' naaghá dóó k'ad 'ashdladiin binááhai lá jiní. Fort Lewis Colorado hoolghéedi 'iíłta' dóó Naat'áanii Néézgi dó' 'iíłta' jiní. 'Ólta yits'áníyáá dóó Colorado bighi' 'akał bistłee'ii ła' yá naalnishgo tseebíí nááhai jiní. 'Áádóó Gad Deelzha hoolghéedi (Mesa Verde) nináánálnishgo tseebííts'áadah nínáánááhai jiní. Bilagáana bitahjí t'éiyá 'aghá naagháá ńt'ę́ę́' jiní, 'áko ndi t'áadoo bidine'é yóó' 'iidíí'ąą da. Bilagáana bitaajigháago t'áadoo le'é bíhojiił'ą́'ąą shįį bee Naabeehó dine'é bee bide'ádahoot'éhígíí binjilnisngo díkwíí shįį ńdoohah. Naabeehó dine'é t'óó 'ahayóí haa dadzólí dóó shįį naat'áanii 'idlįigi hwééhodoozįįł. T'áá bí 'áníigo t'éiyá t'áá 'ii' shéłjaa'ígi bee shidine'é bá ndeeshnish ní jiní.

NAHASDZAAN NAALTSOOS BIKAA' BE'ELYAA

'Anaa' baa na'aldeeh yę́ę́dą́ą́' nihe'ena'í danliinii ha'át'íishįį "rocket" deiłníigo doo deighánígóó nahashkáá' ńdadijahgo 'ádayiilaa lá jiní. 'Éí bee'eldǫǫh bikǫ' yii' hééł 'áńdayiil'įįhgo yee 'ádanihi'niiłdįįd ńt'ę́ę́' lá jiní. 'Áko 'éí bits'ą́ą́' bénálkáá' dóó k'ad nááńáłahgo choo'įįgo 'ályaa jiní. K'ad t'éiyá bee 'ak'inda'a'nilí (camera) biih nát'áahgo deigo dadildon jiní. Deigo hastą́diin dóó ba'aan 'ashdladi tsin sitą́ą́góó 'ánálgho'go 'áádę́ę́' nahasdzáán naaltsoos yik'i niyiinííł jiní.

NAABEEHO ŁA' TIDIILYAA JINI

Díí kwii be'elyaaígíí t'éiyá 'Ahéhéshjįhdi 'ólta'ági 'áhoot'é. Kwii t'áá 'áłaji' shí nahalin. 'Áłchíní doo da'ółta' dago kwii hodootł'izhtahgóó ndaanée łeh. (Ph. courtesy Sherman Inst.)

NAABEEHO LA' DIYOGI YEE HONEESNA

Hoozdo hoolghéedi Arizona State Fair, baa na'aldeeh yę́ę́dą́ą́' Naabeehó 'asdzání Mabel Burnside Myers gholghéé léi' diyogi ch'il bee da'iiltsxóhígíí bee 'ályaago yee honeesná jiní. Mabel Myers t'éiyá Naat'áanii Néezdi 'ólta'ági diyogí 'ál'įįgi bíhoo'aah jiní. Diyogi ts'ídá 'agháadi 'ánoolinígíí dó' yee honeesná jiní.

CHEE DODGE DAATSAAH

Chee Dodge t'áá yéigo daatsaahgo

TSASK'EH BA HOOGHAN DIILTŁA

Hayíiłką́ągo Atlanta Georgia hoolghéedi tsásk'eh bá hooghan ńt'ę́ę́' diiłtła lá jiní. 'Éí Bilagáana t'ááłáhádi neeznádiin dóó ba'aan díįts'áadah yilt'éego nabistseed dóó neeznádiin yilt'éego t'éiyá t'óó tídadiilyaa lá jiní. T'áá

'íídą́ą́' ła' hadádahodeezk'ą́ą́' lágo 'inda kǫ'ígíí hadazdees'įį' jiní. Ła' t'áá 'ákóne dazhdíílid dóó ła' t'éiyá tsésǫ'déé' hadah dahidiijéé'go dazhneezná jiní. Ła' tł'óół 'ádayiilaago yee hadah dahideeshch'ą́ą́ł ńt'ę́ę́' niyolgo biniinaa t'óó hadah 'ahizhneezdee' jiní. Ła' 'áníigo t'éiyá ch'éénísdzid ńt'ę́ę́' diné hadah 'ahinidéehgo yiiłtsą́ ní jiní. 'Éí shįį be'esdzáán yił naa'aashgo dóó t'óó bééhádzidgo nihee honiigaii lá ní jiní. T'óó nihitsiiji' bik'i'deedzá dóó "fan" deiłníigo nitch'i 'ádeiłínígíí haiigiz ní jiní. Diné kǫ' deiniłtsésígíí ła' 'áníigo t'éiyá 'asdzání ła' tsésǫ'dę́ę́' ba'áłchíní naaki

Each new communications technology required new forms of encryption and presented new challenges in decryption. These advances have made the field one that is constantly evolving. Every time a new method of encryption is developed, cryptanalysts (experts in analyzing and breaking codes) must find a way to decrypt messages that use it. Thus, there is a constant battle between those trying to keep secrets and those trying to discover them. Those who succeed as cryptographers are often creative and original thinkers. They may work alone or with a few colleagues, and their work is often secret, especially when it relates to military or political matters. Many cryptographers entered the field because they relish the challenge of solving puzzles. Some were mathematicians, scientists, or technical experts who became code breakers to help protect their countries in times of war or to assist the military's war efforts. This resource tells the stories of some of the men and women who have shaped the field of cryptography, from ancient Rome to the twentieth century. Their stories are the stories of their times, from the wars of the Roman Empire to digital encryption. The codes they created and the codes they broke have shaped human history.

CHAPTER 1

POLYBIUS: CRYPTOGRAPHER OF ROMAN WAR CORRESPONDENCE

Cryptography has played a role in the quest for power and military conquest since ancient times. Cryptographers such as Polybius developed tools that still form the basis for some of the approaches used today.

THE ROMAN CONQUEST OF MACEDONIA

The rulers of Rome continually sought to increase Rome's size and power by conquering territories in Asia, Europe, and Africa. In the Macedonian Wars, the Republic of Rome fought against several large Greek territories. In 179 BCE, the ruler of Macedonia, Philip, died. Philip's son, Perseus, desired to restore Macedonia to a position of power and embarked on a series of attacks against his Greek neighbors. When the Roman Senate heard that Perseus had been involved in an attempt to assassinate one of Rome's allies, it declared war on Macedonia. In 168 BCE, the Roman legions crushed the Macedonian forces at the Battle of Pydna. To help keep the nobles of Macedonia from making further trouble, Rome established a permanent foothold in the area.

A NOBLE HOSTAGE

Polybius's father, Lycortas, was a nobleman of Achaea, a territory in western Greece. It was one of the regions that had signed a nonaggression agreement with Rome, agreeing that the two states would not attack each other. Many of the nobles, including Lycortas, believed that the agreement did not compel Achaea to support Rome militarily, and he advocated for Achaea to remain neutral in the conflict between Rome and Macedonia. After successfully winning the war against Macedonia, Rome did not trust the nobles who had opposed supporting them. They took one thousand Achaean nobles to Rome as hostages to ensure that their families would comply with Roman rule in the future. Among these nobles was Lycortas's son, Polybius. The hostages remained in Rome for seventeen years.

Because he was of noble birth, Polybius was highly educated and cultured. Therefore, he was welcomed into the circles of Roman nobles. Polybius became particularly close to Lucius Aemilius Paulus Macedonicus, the Roman general who had won the Macedonian War (168 BCE). Aemilius asked Polybius to oversee the education of his sons Fabius and Scipio Aemilianus.

Even after Scipio Aemilianus grew up, he continued to rely on Polybius for advice. The Achaean hostages

Polybius was tutor to Scipio Aemilianus, who would eventually become an acclaimed Roman general. Polybius developed the means to send encrypted military messages while accompanying him on campaign.

were freed in 150 BCE. However, instead of returning home, Polybius chose to accompany Scipio as counselor when Rome undertook the Third Punic War (149–146 BCE). Scipio was given charge of the Roman forces and defeated the Carthaginians in Phoenicia, an area along the coast of what is now Lebanon, Israel, and Syria. Later that year, Polybius went home to Greece. He became active in the government and implemented changes in the way the country was ruled.

JULIUS CAESAR: SECRET WRITING

Julius Caesar (100 BCE–44 BCE) was a renowned Roman general who rose to become emperor of Rome. In conducting his military campaigns, he used ciphers to keep his messages secret. A cipher is a means of replacing the letters that make up a message, one letter at a time. In contrast, a code replaces entire words or phrases to conceal the meaning of the content. For example, the phrase "Uncle Oliver will be going to a ballgame at noon" might mean "The president will be arriving at Congress at noon." One method used by Caesar is known as the Caesar cipher. It is a simple substitution cipher in which the positions of letters are transposed; for example, if every letter in the alphabet was replaced with a letter two spaces to the right:

abcdefghijklmnopqrstuvwxyz
cdefghijklmnopqrstuvwxyzab

"hello" would become "khnnq."

Caesar also used more sophisticated methods. In one case, he needed to get a message to one of his officers, Cicero, who was besieged and could not be reached by a messenger. Caesar needed to let him know that he should not surrender because reinforcements were nearby. Caesar wrote the message in Latin, but instead of using the Roman alphabet, he used Greek letters that represented the same sound as the corresponding Latin ones. Thus, if the

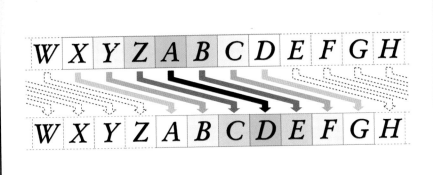

In Caesar's alphabetic substitution cipher each letter is replaced by a different letter a certain number of spaces to the right, in this case, three spaces to the right.

enemy got hold of the message and attempted to read the Greek, it would appear to be nonsense. Caesar had an archer attach the message to an arrow and shoot it into the embattled fortress. A soldier found it and brought the message to Cicero. When Cicero read the message aloud, its meaning was crystal clear. Caesar always used some sort of code or cipher to obscure the meaning of any message he wanted to remain secret.

Polybius wrote a well-known series of histories. His observation of military conflict made it clear that an army needed a way to transmit secret messages from a distance to convey orders and information. Polybius developed a cipher that made it possible to accomplish this feat. A cipher substitutes other letters (or numbers) for the letters that make up the words in

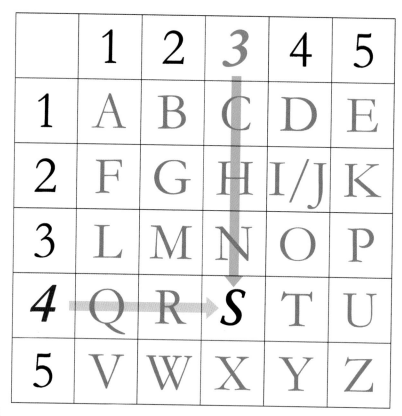

In the Polybius square, the letters of the alphabet are written in a grid. The numbers of the row and column that intersect at a letter are used to represent that letter.

a message. Today, the technique that Polybius instituted is known as the Polybius square.

THE POLYBIUS SQUARE

The Polybius square consists of a five-by-five grid of letters. The letters of the alphabet are arranged left to right, top to bottom (when using the English twenty-six-letter alphabet, the letters "j" and "l" are combined). Five numbers are listed in a row above the letters and five numbers are listed down the left side of the grid. Each letter is represented by the two numbers that intersect.

Thus, in this simple grid, 1-1 represents "A," and 2-3 represents "M." The Polybius square lends itself to telegraphy, sending messages without delivering a physical object such as a letter. In *The Histories*, Polybius describes how his cipher could be used to send messages by using raised and lowered torches, which could easily be seen at a distance. The Polybius cipher can be used with a variety of devices, including sound—from horns or drums, for instance—or smoke signals. The Polybius square can also be used to encipher written messages, as long as both parties know the arrangement of the letters and numbers in the grid. The Polybius square allows the sending of detailed messages, which is a considerable advance over early methods of signaling that were limited to prearranged signals. (For example, Paul Revere's lantern signal "one if by land, two if by sea.") Later variations of the Polybius cipher for written messages include replacing the five numbers with a five-letter keyword.

CHAPTER 2

BLAISE DE VIGENÈRE: THE VIGENÈRE CIPHER

During the Renaissance (1400s–1600s), European powers vied with one another for power and territory. This war was fought on diplomatic as well as military fronts. Intrigue was everywhere, and keeping diplomatic messages secret was important. Blaise de Vigenère (1523–1596) is the most famous cryptographer of the Renaissance.

A TIME OF INTRIGUE

Throughout the Renaissance, the countries of Europe competed with one another for military, political, economic, territorial, and religious dominance. This battling resulted in constantly shifting alliances and rivalries. For the first time, a class of professional diplomats arose. Consuls and ambassadors, their staffs, and resident agents based in foreign countries all acted as representatives of the European rulers. Other official diplomats traveled to various

Blaise de Vigenère devised a form of cryptography that used a polyalphabetic cipher and a key.

countries as needed. Blaise de Vigenère was such a diplomat. In addition to conveying messages from the rulers of their own countries, diplomats secretly reported on the activities of the governments of the countries where they were located. A great deal of the information they sent could result in scandal, strained relations, or even war, if the wrong people intercepted their messages. In addition, a messenger might—willingly or unwillingly—reveal important information, so cryptography became a critical tool for diplomats.

THE MAKING OF A DIPLOMAT

Blaise de Vigenère was born to a noble family in Saint-Pourçain on Sioule, in France. His father had him educated in Paris, where he entered the diplomatic service at the age of seventeen and contin-

Leon Battista Alberti applied math to cryptography, developing the concept of a polyalphabetic cipher and creating a cipher disk for an early form of mechanical encryption.

ued to serve for thirty years. When he was twenty-four, Vigenère went to work for the Duke of Nevers, who was secretary of the King's Chamber for diplomacy. In the duke's service, he made many trips to Italy, Germany, and the Netherlands. In 1549, he visited Rome on a two-year diplomatic mission and undertook another mission to Rome in 1566. Keeping messages secret was always a concern in diplomatic circles, and Vigenère was fascinated with codes and ciphers. In Rome, he read books about cryptography, including works by the fifteenth-century scholars Trithemius and Alberti, and the sixteenth-century cryptologist Bellaso. These writers described polyalphabetic ciphers— ciphers that use more than one alphabet to encrypt messages. Earlier scholars had noted a polyalphabetic means by which messages could be encoded, but the resulting cipher was easy to break. After Vigenère retired in 1570, he worked out such a system of encoding, using a polyalphabetic cipher and a key, which made messages more difficult to decode. The resulting method is now known as the Vigenère cipher.

THE VIGENÈRE CIPHER

Vigenère published his concept in a work called *Traicté des chiffres, ou, Secrètes manières d'escrire* (Tract on ciphers, or secret ways to write). He explained a new way to employ a form of encoding described by Johannes Trimethius (1462–1516), called a Trimethius table. A Trimethius table lays out the letters of an alphabet in a series of rows. Each row is shifted by one letter:

a b c d e f g h i j k l m n o p q r s t u v w x y z
b c d e f g h i j k l m n o p q r s t u v w x y z a
c d e f g h i j k l m n o p q r s t u v w x y z a b
(and so on)

Any of the lines can be used to encrypt a message. The person encrypting a message takes the first letter on

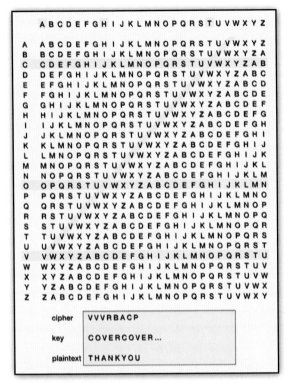

This illustration of the Vigenère cipher, uses "Vvvrbacp" as the cipher and "Covercover" as the key, resulting in "thank you" as the message.

the first row and replaces it with the letter in the same column on the chosen line. For example, if the second line is used, "bad" becomes "cbe." This type of code is easily broken, however, because the letters in words still occur with the same frequency as in normal usage. Giovan Battista Bellaso had improved on this basic method by introducing the idea of a keyword, such as the first word of the message, to indicate which line to use to encode each letter in a message. Thus, if the first word of the message is "Attack," the line beginning with "a" would be used first, then the line beginning with "t," and so on. Vigenère further enhanced the system by introducing the concept of a keyword unrelated to the message to create a more powerful encryption method. In his method, a keyword is selected and a person uses the rows that start with each letter of the keyword to encrypt the message. For example, if the keyword is "circus" and the text is "attack tonight," then

Antoine Rossignol and the "Black Chamber"

Antoine Rossignol (1600–1682) was a French mathematician. In 1626, the French government forces were besieging the city of Réalmont, which was held by dissident Huguenots (French Protestants). Rossignol decoded a message carried by a messenger who was captured when leaving the city. The document revealed that the city was running out of supplies and ammunition, which allowed the French to demand its surrender. This incident brought Rossignol to the attention of the French king, Louis XIII. Cardinal Richelieu, the king's chief minister, employed Rossignol repeatedly to decipher coded information. Rossignol's ability to rapidly decrypt messages made him important to Richelieu's intelligence and diplomatic operations. Rossignol worked extensively for Louis XIII and later Louis XIV. He improved the methods used by the government to encrypt messages as well as to decrypt them, creating *Le grand chiffre* ("The Great Cipher") with his son, Bonaventure, around 1650 for Louis XIV's use. Rossignol also expanded the country's decryption efforts, eventually creating an organization of cryptanalysts for the government, which he dubbed the *cabinet noir* (the "Black Chamber"). The Black Chamber was so successful that the governments of other countries in Europe implemented their own "black chambers," and the term became a universal term for government cryptographic organizations.

This is the title page of the first edition of Vigenère's Traicté des chiffres *(Tract on Ciphers), in which he describes his method for encrypting messages using a cipher and key.*

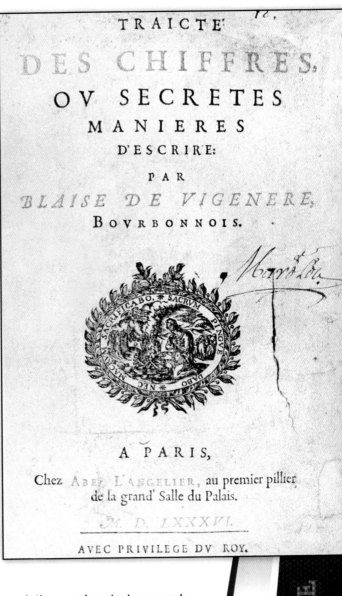

the keyword tells the writer which line to use to encode each letter of the message.

The line starting with "c" is used to encode the first letter of the message, the line beginning with "i" is utilized to encode the second letter of the message, and so on. When all six letters of "circus" have been used, the sender starts over at the beginning of the word. This technique of employing a keyword, called key scheduling, is used today as part of the Data Encryption Standard (DES), which is utilized for the encryption of messages that are sent electronically via computers.

CHAPTER 3

ANSON STAGER: CIVIL WAR CRYPTOGRAPHY

In 1844, the industrial age brought a novel technology for transmitting messages—the telegraph. In 1861, the American Civil War started and the telegraph became a military communication tool. The telegraph required a new kind of expert in cryptography. That expert was Anson Stager.

A REVOLUTION IN TECHNOLOGY

Samuel Morse patented the electrical telegraph system in 1837. Telegraph systems allowed messages to be transmitted nearly instantaneously between distant points, vastly improving the sharing of information. To send a message, an operator presses a key, which transmits an electric signal that travels down an electric wire strung between poles, much like the power lines one sees today. The signal produces a sound at the receiving end. To allow messages to be transmitted, Morse devised a system in which each letter is represented by a series of short and long pulses (dots and dashes). The receiving operator translates them back into the individual letters. This series of dots and dashes is known as Morse Code. By October 1861, telegraph lines extended across the United States, and telegraphy became the main means of transmitting long-distance messages, replacing the Pony Express.

When the Civil War broke out in 1861, the telegraph system made it possible to instantaneously transmit orders and military intelligence to both Confederate and Union generals in the field. However, to transmit messages, telegraph operators had to read them, which made the messages insecure. In addition, because Morse Code was generally known, if the messages were intercepted, they could easily be understood. Therefore, the Union Military Telegraph Department had a pressing need for a method of encrypting the messages to ensure their secrecy. They turned to Anson Stager.

An 1865 photograph shows Anson Stager in his role as Brevet Brigadier General of the US Army Telegraph Corps during the US Civil War.

MASTER OF THE TELEGRAPH

Anson Stager (1825–1885) was born in Ontario, New York. At age sixteen, he began working as a printer's apprentice. He subsequently went to work for Henry O'Reilly, a telegraph builder in Rochester, New York. When O'Reilly built telegraph lines across Pennsylvania in 1846, he put twenty-one-year-old Stager in charge of the Lancaster, Pennsylvania, telegraph office. Two years later,

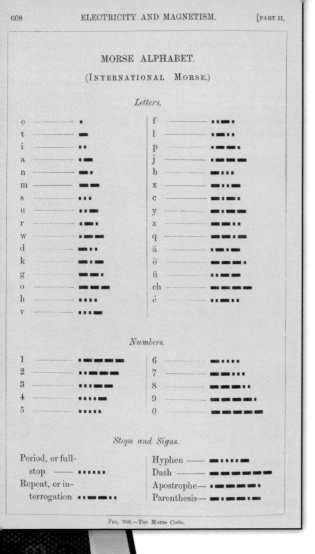

MORSE ALPHABET.

(INTERNATIONAL MORSE.)

Letters.

e	▪	f	▪▪▬▪
t	▬	l	▪▬▪▪
i	▪▪	p	▪▬▬▪
a	▪▬	j	▪▬▬▬
n	▬▪	b	▬▪▪▪
m	▬▬	x	▬▪▪▬
s	▪▪▪	c	▬▪▬▪
u	▪▪▬	y	▬▪▬▬
r	▪▬▪	z	▬▬▪▪
w	▪▬▬	q	▬▬▪▬
d	▬▪▪	ä	▪▬▪▬
k	▬▪▬	ö	▬▬▬▪
g	▬▬▪	ü	▪▪▬▬
o	▬▬▬	ch	▬▬▬▬
h	▪▪▪▪	é	▪▪▬▪▪
v	▪▪▪▬		

Numbers.

1	▪▬▬▬▬	6	▬▪▪▪▪
2	▪▪▬▬▬	7	▬▬▪▪▪
3	▪▪▪▬▬	8	▬▬▬▪▪
4	▪▪▪▪▬	9	▬▬▬▬▪
5	▪▪▪▪▪	0	▬▬▬▬▬

Stops and Signs.

Period, or full-stop	▪▪▪▪▪▪	Hyphen	▬▪▪▪▪▬
Repeat, or in-terrogation	▪▪▬▬▪▪	Dash	▬▬▬▬▬
		Apostrophe	▪▬▬▬▬▪
		Parenthesis	▬▪▬▬▪▬

Fig. 380.—The Morse Code.

This page shows the alphabet represented in Morse code. Each letter is sent as a combination of long and short electrical pulses (dots and dashes).

Stager became chief operator of the national lines based in Cincinnati, Ohio. When Western Union was formed in 1856, he became the company's first general superintendent.

When the Civil War began, the governor of Ohio asked Stager to come up with a cipher that could be used to send communications related to the defense of the Midwest via telegraph. The cipher came to the attention of Major-General George B. McClellan of the Union army, who asked Stager to take charge of the Military Telegraph Department, employing his ciphers. Stager remained in this position until 1868 and was made a brevet brigadier general of volunteers in return for his service.

THE STAGER CIPHER

Called upon by the US government to develop a means of encoding military messages in which the code could not be easily broken, Stager developed a new type of

American Telegraph Company,

BALTIMORE AND CINCINNATI DIVISION.

Connecting with the Company's Lines at Baltimore, and with the Lines of the Western Union Company at Cincinnati.

MESSAGES RECEIVED FOR AND TRANSMITTED TO ALL STATIONS IN THE UNITED STATES AND BRITISH PROVINCES.

TERMS AND CONDITIONS ON WHICH THIS AND ALL MESSAGES ARE RECEIVED BY THIS COMPANY FOR TRANSMISSION.

In order to guard against errors or delays in the transmission or delivery of messages, every message of importance ought to be REPEATED by being sent back from the station at which it is to be received to the station from which it is originally sent. Half the usual price for transmission will be charged for repeating the message, and while this Company will, as heretofore, use every precaution to ensure correctness, it will not be responsible for errors or delays in the transmission or delivery of repeated messages beyond FIFTY dollars, unless a special agreement for insurance be made and paid for at the time of sending the message, and the amount of risk specified on this agreement; nor is the Company to be responsible for any error or delay in the transmission or delivery or non-delivery of any unrepeated message, BEYOND FIVE DOLLARS, unless in like manner specially insured and amount of risk paid for at the time. No liability is assumed for any error or neglect by any other Company over whose lines this message may be sent to reach its destination. No liability for any errors in cipher messages.

CAMBRIDGE LIVINGSTON, Sec'y,
145 BROADWAY, N. Y.

E. S. SANFORD, Pres't,
145 BROADWAY, N. Y.

3. Dated _____ 1862.

Rec'd, _____ 1862 _____ o'clock _____ min. M.

To _____

Can angels Co-operate Cut
a also protect position
End time this the Cheat
What form from are
devils so off force to
the on pleasant finis

I D Cox.
Maj Genl Comdg.

This 1862 message was written in Stager cipher. The handwritten message would have been rewritten into a grid by the recipient so that it could be decoded with a code book.

Auguste Kerckhoffs: Keeping Military Secrets

Although military messages in the 1800s were often encoded, the codes used were simple and often easily broken. Auguste Kerckhoffs (1835–1903) was a Dutch cryptographer and professor of languages at a school in Paris. In 1883, he wrote an essay, titled "La cryptographie militaire" ("Military Cryptography"), which was published in two installments in *Militaires (Journal of Military Science)*. In this work, he laid out six basic requirements of cryptography:

1. The system must be indecipherable in practice (even if it is theoretically possible to decode it mathematically).

2. It must not rely on secrecy to work. Even if a message falls into the enemy's hands, the enemy must not be able to understand the message. In other words, you need a specific key to decode a message.

3. The key used to decode the cipher must be able to be communicated without relying on written notes, and it must be possible for the correspondents to change it at will.

4. It should be possible to use it for telegraphic communications.

5. The necessary equipment or documents must be easily portable and not require many people to use.

6. Finally, it should be easy for people to use and not require extreme mental skill or knowledge of a large number of rules.

These rules still apply to cryptography today (if one substitutes "computer" for "telegraph"). The second of these principles is known as Kerckhoffs's principle. The central idea is that the key, not secrecy about the coding method, is what keeps a coded message secure. Thus, even if everything about a coding system is known except the key necessary to decode a message, the message should still be secure. This principle still forms the basis of modern encryption methods for messages transmitted via electronic devices.

cipher—a transportation cipher. In this type of cipher, the order of the words in a message is changed, or transposed. The words in the message are written out in lines arranged above each other and then the message is rewritten arranging the words by column instead of by line. Stager continued to enhance the technique, adding code words with predetermined meanings for the message and using different paths through the columns of words to make the cipher more difficult to break. The fact that Stager's method of encryption used recognizable words made it easier for telegraph operators to send the content without errors, while the mixing of the words in the message made it incomprehensible if intercepted. The Confederates did intercept Union messages encoded with Stager's ciphers, but they were never able to break the code. In contrast, the Confederates relied primarily on the Vigenère cipher, which led to a large number of errors in transmission and ultimately allowed cryptanalysts working for President Abraham Lincoln to break the Confederate code.

Chapter 4

Agnes Meyer Driscoll, aka Madame X

A t the time that World War I (1914–1918) began, the telegraph was used extensively to send military intelligence information and orders. However, technology continued to advance, and by the last years of the war, radio had become a standard means of communication in the field. Both telegraphic and radio messages were subject to interception. Therefore, messages were sent in encrypted form—and the success or failure of participants in a war could depend on their skill in decrypting them.

The War to End All Wars

World War I started in Europe on July 28, 1914, a month after the assassination of Archduke Franz Ferdinand of Austria by a Serbian nationalist. Austria-Hungary declared war on Serbia. The Russians mobilized troops in support of Serbia. Germany invaded neutral Belgium and Luxembourg, moving toward France. The United Kingdom (UK) declared war on Germany in support of France. The war started in Europe but quickly expanded, as more and more countries joined the conflict. On one side, the major powers were the UK and its empire, France, and the Russian Empire (the Allies). On the other side were Germany and Austria-Hungary (the Central Powers). Eventually, Japan and the United States joined the Allies, and the Ottoman Empire and Bulgaria joined the Central Powers. In total, more than seventy million members of the various militaries were involved, and in excess of nine million military combatants and seven million civilians were killed. The results of the conflict were so devastating that people dubbed the conflict "the war to end all wars."

MADAME X

Agnes Meyer Driscoll (1889–1971), code-named Madame X, worked for the US government during World War I and World War II. She was an exceptional cryptanalyst and a pioneer in cryptographic techniques and equipment. Born Agnes May Meyer in Geneseo, Illinois, she moved with her family to Westerville, Ohio, in 1895. She majored in mathematics and physics at Ohio State University, from which she graduated in 1911 with a bachelor's degree. She also studied foreign

Agnes Meyer Driscoll, also known as Madame X, excelled as a cryptanalyst during both World War I and World War II.

languages, music, and statistics and spoke French, German, and Japanese fluently. After graduating, she moved to Amarillo, Texas, where she became director of music at a military academy and later head of the mathematics department at Amarillo High School.

In January 1917, the British government intercepted and decrypted a telegram from the German foreign office proposing an alliance between Germany and Mexico against the United States. In response, the United States declared war on Germany. The American entry into World War I changed Agnes Meyer's life. The armed forces quickly absorbed the available pool of men, and by the beginning of 1918, the US Navy, finding itself short of personnel, decided to allow women to enlist. Agnes Meyer enlisted in June 1918 with the rank of chief yeoman, the highest rank available to a woman. For most of her career, she worked for the Code and Signal Section under the Director of Naval Communications (DNC). This section was responsible for developing the navy's ciphers and codes. The war ended in 1918, but navy women were offered the option of continuing to work for the navy as civilians. Agnes Meyer took the opportunity to do so and continued to work for the navy in the same capacity (with the exception of a two-year break to work for a private company) until 1949.

Breaking Codes and Ciphers

At the end of World War I, the navy's effort to intercept and decrypt radio messages was still in its infancy. Agnes Meyer spent a year working with Lieutenant Commander William Gresham, head of the Code and Signal Section, to develop a machine that could be used to create ciphers. In 1921, they produced the Communications Machine (CM). This piece of equipment, which used a varying alphabet system, was the navy's primary encryption device throughout the 1920s. In 1937, Congress awarded Agnes

GEORGES-JEAN PAINVIN: ADFGVX

Georges-Jean Painvin (1886–1980) studied at a mining college in France and then became a lecturer in geology and paleontology. Early in World War I, he became friendly with a cryptologist for France's Sixth Army and did some work on a cipher. Impressed by his work, the Bureau de Chiffres invited him to work for them on breaking German codes. In March 1918, the German Army was preparing for a major assault, designed to separate the French and British forces and take the area around Amiens. They used a code that was called the ADFGVX cipher because the messages sent with the cipher consisted of these six letters. The cipher combined a Polybius square with transposition of the columns of letters to create a cipher that was very difficult to break. Painvin studied eighteen encrypted communications, observing patterns in the messages and analyzing the number of times various letters occurred in columns. After four days and nights of work, he finally broke the cipher, and the information revealed assisted the Allies in foiling the German attack. After the war, Painvin returned to the

Georges-Jean Painvin broke the German ADFGVX code in World War I.

mining field and became the president of several companies. His war work was not revealed until much later. He was made a knight of the French Legion of Honor in 1933 and a grand officer of the order in 1973.

Meyer Driscoll $15,000 (equivalent to roughly $250,000 in 2016 dollars) in recognition of her work.

In 1924, Agnes Meyer married Michael B. Driscoll, a lawyer for the Department of Commerce. In the mid-1920s, she became the crypt-analyst for a navy code-breaking mission led by Lieutenant Laurance Safford, called the Research Desk, where she worked for eighteen years. Driscoll broke the code used by the Japanese Imperial Navy in their Red Book, and later, in the 1930s, the Japanese Blue Book codes. She also broke the codes pro-duced by the M-1, or Orange, cipher machine used by the Japanese naval attachés. In 1940, she did significant work on the Japanese fleet's operational code, JN-25, but her efforts were interrupted when she was transferred to the US team working to break the German Enigma code after the United States declared war on Germany in World War II. In 1948, she joined the newly created Armed Forces Security Agency, and in 1952, the National Security Agency (NSA). She retired in 1959. When she died in 1971, she was buried in Arlington National Cemetery. In 2000, the NSA inducted her into its Hall of Honor.

CHAPTER 5

ELIZEBETH FRIEDMAN: GANGSTERS AND SPIES

The use of coded messages was not limited to the military. They were also employed by criminals, including gangsters who smuggled alcohol during Prohibition. Elizebeth Friedman's role was to crack those codes.

BETWEEN THE WARS

In 1920, the US government passed the Eighteenth Amendment to the US Constitution, which prohibited the manufacturing, storage, transportation,

Cryptanalyst Elizebeth Friedman headed the first FBI/Coast Guard unit dedicated to cryptanalysis.

sale, possession, and consumption of alcohol. This amendment ushered in a period known as Prohibition. Prohibition would last until 1933, when it was repealed by the Twenty-First Amendment. To enforce Prohibition, Congress passed the Volstead Act, which spelled out the penalties for violating the Eighteenth Amendment and gave law enforcement the power to arrest people for violating it. Many Americans were not prepared to give up drinking alcohol, however. The result was the rise of an illicit trade in the importation and sale of liquor. The business brought in huge sums of money, resulting in the rise of large operations run by gangsters. The US Treasury Department was charged with preventing the smuggling of alcohol into the United States. The US Coast Guard ensured compliance with maritime regulations and enforced customs regulations, which included combating smuggling and piracy. To avoid detection of their activities, the gangsters resorted to codes and ciphers.

ALCOHOL, DRUGS, AND GUNS

Elizebeth Smith was the youngest of nine children. Her father was a successful dairy farmer in Indiana. Smith graduated from Hillsdale College in 1913 with a degree in English. In 1916, she started working for Riverbank, in Illinois, a private research facility run by George Fabyan, a wealthy businessman. Her initial job at Riverbank was to analyze the works of Shakespeare to establish whether Sir Francis Bacon had written them. At Riverbank, she met William Friedman, who collaborated with her on the project.

Fabyan convinced the US government to use Riverbank's cryptanalysts to break codes for the War Department during World War I. Elizebeth and William both worked on the project. They married in 1917. After the war, in 1921, the War Department asked the couple to move to Washington, DC, and continue to work as cryptanalysts. William had started in the Army's Signal Corps and would eventually become a lieutenant colonel and the chief cryptologist of the Department of Defense. Elizebeth joined the Treasury Department. Elizebeth Friedman decoded more than twelve thousand messages and was instrumental in the capture and conviction of many smugglers.

In one case, she helped the United States in an incident with Canada. A boat called *I'm Alone*, registered in Canada, was spotted off the coast of Louisiana on March 20, 1929. The US Coast Guard knew the ship had recently been loaded with liquor in Belize. The Coast Guard tracked the *I'm Alone*, and on March 22, two Coast Guard boats trapped the *I'm Alone* 220 miles (354 kilometers) from the Gulf Coast. They opened fire, shooting up the hull and the Canadian flag on the masthead. All the crewmembers except one man were rescued. The fact that the Coast Guard had fired on a Canadian ship angered the Canadian government, which claimed that the US government owed them $386,803 for the ship, its cargo, and the personnel lost. Elizebeth Friedman set out to decode twenty-three messages sent from Belize to a contact in New York. Successfully breaking the cipher used by the conspirators, she was able to prove that, although the *I'm Alone* was registered in Canada, it was owned by Americans—and they intended to smuggle liquor.

Because she proved that the American forces had fired on an American ship, the arbitrators assigned by the court made the decision to reduce the judgment to a

Federal agents pour barrels of wine into the gutter outside the Federal Building in Los Angeles in 1920. Prohibition forbade the making, storing, and selling of alcohol.

$50,665 fine to the Canadian government, along with a public apology for firing on the Canadian flag.

In 1930, Elizebeth Friedman was able to convince the Treasury Department to set up a permanent cryptanalysis unit in the Coast Guard. Friedman became head of a six-person office. Her unit intercepted and decoded radio messages that enabled federal agents to raid the New Orleans headquarters of a Canadian-based liquor-smuggling ring. They issued warrants for more than one hundred people, including four members of gangster Al Capone's gang.

To Catch a Spy

Prohibition ended in 1933, but a new danger was on the horizon. Actions by the German government in Europe led to the outbreak of World War II (1939–1945). The Japanese allied themselves with Germany and posed a threat to the West Coast of the United States. Elizabeth Friedman was instrumental in the capture of a notorious spy for the Japanese, Velvalee Dickinson. She was born Velvalee Malvena Blucher in Sacramento, California, and graduated from Stanford University. She worked at a San Francisco investment firm from the late 1920s to the mid-1930s. She married the owner of the firm, Lee T. Dickinson. The firm had Japanese-American clients, and the Dickinsons became supporters of Japanese-American relations. They joined the Japanese-American Society and were guests at the Japanese consulate. When the investment firm suffered a downturn in 1937, the Dickinsons moved to New York, where Velvalee opened a doll shop—and became a spy for Japan. Selling dolls to collectors both in the United States and abroad provided her with a cover for her espionage activities. She was known as the doll woman. She wrote to Japanese agents, using the names and addresses of her customers as return addresses. When several letters she sent to a Japanese contact in Buenos Aires, Argentina, could not be delivered, they were returned by the post office to the woman

Friendman works with colleague Robert Gordon at a desk decoding documents in 1940.

whose return address was on them. She turned them over to the FBI as suspicious, and Elizebeth Friedman was able to decode them to reveal that they contained information about US naval defenses and ships—in

HERBERT OSBORN YARDLEY: THE AMERICAN BLACK CHAMBER

Herbert Osborn Yardley was born in 1889 in Worthington, Indiana. As a young man, he studied for a year at the University of Chicago before becoming a clerk and telegrapher in the US State Department's code room. Instead of merely transmitting code messages, he began trying to see if he could break them. When he did so, he issued a one-hundred-page document, and the system was improved—but not to his satisfaction. When the United States entered World War I, he became a first lieutenant in the Reserve Officer Corps and was put in charge of forming a new organization: MI-8, the cryptographic branch of US military intelligence.

Yardley's organization, informally called the American Black Chamber, analyzed all types of secret messages, including encryptions, ciphers, codes, and documents written with secret inks. It decrypted messages intercepted by radio listening stations and military field units, as well as material sent by the Federal Bureau of Investigation (FBI). By the end of the war in 1918, MI-8 employed 18 officers, 24 civilian cryptographers, and 109 typists and stenographers. The organization decrypted forty-five thousand messages. However, the organization was disbanded by President Herbert Hoover in 1929 as part of his efforts to create a new atmosphere of international trust among nations.

particular, information about the US naval fleet at Pearl Harbor, Hawaii. The FBI established that the addresses used on the letters all belonged to customers of the doll shop. The cryptanalysis provided by Elizebeth Friedman led to an indictment of Velvalee Dickinson. She eventually pleaded guilty. Elizebeth Friedman retired in 1946. In 1957, she and William published the results of their Shakespearean research, which supported the conclusion that Shakespeare had written his plays himself. She died in 1980.

CHAPTER 6
ALAN TURING: SOLVING ENIGMA

World War II (1939–1945) brought rapid advances in technology on many fronts, and the Germans were at the forefront of much of that development. Their use of the Enigma machine resulted in a seemingly unbreakable code.

THE ENIGMA CODE

During World War II, the Germans used coded radio messages to send orders to their forces. British intelligence intercepted many of the German messages but intelligence officers were unable to decode them. The British knew that breaking those codes was the key to winning the war.

The Germans used a series of electromechanical cipher machines, brand-named Enigma, to generate their messages. The typical machine contained rotating cylinders. After choosing a series of letters, an operator rotated the cylinders, which produced random letters to replace the original series. Because the cylinders generated so many possible combinations of letters, which were always different, the only way to break the code was for the person who received the message to duplicate the original series of cylinder rotations, which was almost impossible. The earliest version of the Enigma machine used three cylinders, but the Germans kept improving the machine and adding more cylinders. By 1941, the Germans could encode messages 1.8×10^{20} different ways using Enigma.

At the beginning of World War II, in 1939, the British government moved its code-breaking organization, the Government Code and Cipher School,

This Enigma machine from the 1930s had three rotors that turned, generating random letters to replace those in the message being encrypted.

from London to an estate in Buckinghamshire called Bletchley Park. The staff consisted of both mathematicians and people who were good at solving codes and puzzles.

ALAN TURING

Among the mathematicians whom the British government employed to break the Enigma code was Alan Turing of Cambridge University. Alan Turing (1912–1954) was born in London. He graduated from Cambridge University in England in 1934 and obtained a PhD from Princeton University in 1938. When he was twenty-four, he published a paper in which he explored the concept of using machines to perform logical functions. Many consider him the father of computer science because his papers describe many of the concepts that were later used in computer technology. In 1937, Turing designed "the Turing machine," a hypothetical machine that could manipulate symbols on a strip of paper according to rules that it was given. Today people call this programming. These rules that tell computers what to do are called algorithms.

PHILIP JOHNSTON: THE NAVAJO CODE TALKERS

Radio technology, still in its infancy during World War I, had developed into a staple of the military by the start of World War II. The military used portable radio sets with metal casing in the field to transmit and receive information and orders. During engagements between the United States and Japan in the small islands of the Pacific, information in the field had to be transmitted in minutes—or even seconds—as situations changed. The electromagnetic cipher machines used to encrypt US messages were too slow, but when soldiers resorted to speaking plain English, they revealed valuable information to the Japanese. Philip Johnston (1892–1978) had an idea for a way to employ an unbreakable code that would allow messages to be transmitted immediately: use a unique language. This concept was the foundation for the Navajo code talkers.

Two Navajo code talkers with the US Army in the Pacific during World War II relay information from the field. Few people spoke Navajo, so the Japanese couldn't decode the messages.

Johnston was a Los Angeles–based engineer. Because his father was a missionary, he had grown up near a Navajo reservation in Arizona and learned to speak Navajo. He was often called on to translate between the Navajo and government representatives. Aware that Navajo was incomprehensible to those outside the tribe, Johnston went to the head of the Marine signal office in San Diego, Lieutenant Colonel James E. Jones, and suggested that each unit in the field should employ a pair of Navajos as radio operators. They would be able to send real-time messages to one another in Navajo, with no delay for encryption and decryption. Jones was taken with Johnston's proposal and demonstration, and a pilot program was established with thirty-three Navajo men, from age fifteen and up. The Navajo language lacked terms for modern military technology, so a lexicon was created in which Navajo words were substituted for military terms. For example, the word "hummingbird" was used for "fighter plane," "war chief" was used for "commander," and "mustache smeller" meant "Adolf Hitler." In addition, a set of standard words was used to spell out terms for which an equivalent had not already been established. For instance, the Navajo words that translated to English words starting with *P, A, C, I,* and *F* were used to represent the letters that spelled out "Pacific." Of course, the spelling was clear only if one knew what the Navajo words translated to in English because they didn't start with the same letters as the English words. The project was so successful that it was expanded to include 420 Navajo men. Navajo code talkers took part in every major assault in the Pacific theater of the war, serving with every Marine division. The Navajo code was never broken.

DEMYSTIFYING ENIGMA

Alan Turing 1912–1954
Mathematician and WWII code breaker

The key to solving the Enigma code was to reproduce the sequence of rotations of the cylinders in the Enigma machine. To do this, Turing designed an electromechanical device dubbed the British Bombe at Bletchley Park. Multiple bombes were built. Each one measured about 7 feet (2.1 meters) wide,

Seen here in a postage stamp, the British Bombe machine devised by Alan Turing contained rows of disks, which rotated in order to mirror the combinations of letters used in the Enigma code.

6 feet 6 inches (1.98 m) tall, and 2 feet (0.61 m) deep. Mounted on each bombe were three groups of twelve drums. The drums were arranged in triplets to mirror the three rotors of an Enigma scrambler. Turing used an electrical circuit to automate the rotation of the drums. It took about twenty minutes for the bombe to cycle through all the positions to which a rotor could be set.

The problem was that to decode a specific message, Turing needed to give the machine a decoded word for the initial setting. The breakthrough came when it was recognized that every message started with certain types of phrases, such as the weather report. The machine could use such phrases as a crib (a word whose encrypted letters were known) to test the combinations of encoded letters and come up with the solution to decoding the message. As a result of the bombe, the British were able to decode German messages and learn of Germany's plans in advance, allowing them to take appropriate counteractions.

After the war, Turing went to work for the National Physical Laboratory. He designed the Automated Computing Engine (ACE), which was one of the earliest concepts for a stored-program computer (a computer that can store a series of instructions in memory). He later worked on some of the earliest programmable computers at Manchester University. One of his best-known concepts is the Turing

Alan Turing is deemed by many to be the father of computer science. He headed the effort to break the Enigma code.

Test. The test says that a computer is "intelligent" if a human being interacting with it can't tell that it is a computer.

In 1952, Turing was arrested for being homosexual, which was against the law in England at that time. He was forced to undergo a traumatic treatment as an alternative to going to prison. Two years later, just before he turned forty-two, Turing died of cyanide poisoning. His death is often attributed to suicide, but some who were close to him believe that it may have been an accident. In 2009, the British government publicly apologized for the way Turing had been treated, and Prime Minister Gordon Brown acknowledged Turing's contribution to "Britain's fight against the darkness of dictatorship."

CHAPTER 7

WHITFIELD DIFFIE AND MARTIN HELLMAN: PUBLIC-KEY CRYPTOGRAPHY

The advent of digital communication meant that securing information was no longer a problem for governments and military organizations only, but also for the general public. Individuals and businesses needed a way to protect their personal and business information as it traveled electronically from source to destination. What was needed was a way to encrypt information on the sending side and decrypt it on the receiving side without having to physically deliver a secret key. The developers of that technology were Whitfield Diffie, Martin Hellman, and Ralph Merkle in the United States and James Ellis in the United Kingdom.

Whitfield Diffie developed the concept of public-key cryptography, which allows communications to be sent via computer securely.

Public-Key Cryptography

Encrypting electronic communications is similar to encrypting written messages, except that a computer performs the encryption. A computer puts the communications through a series of changes, using a key to decide which changes to make. The problem is that to decrypt the message, the receiver needs to have the key. So how does one securely transmit the key to the receiver without allowing someone else to intercept it? At first, banks and the government sent couriers to physically deliver a set of keys to be used for a set period, but this was impractical and too expensive for the general public and most businesses. For decades, the problem seemed insurmountable. However, in the 1970s, researchers came up with a revolutionary solution. Their breakthrough is considered by many to be one of the most important achievements in the field of cryptography.

A Meeting of Minds

Whitfield Diffie was born in 1944 in Washington, DC, but grew up in New York, where his father was a professor at the City College of New York. He was interested in mathematics from the time he was a child. In 1965, he graduated from the Massachusetts Institute of Technology (MIT) with a bachelor's degree in mathematics and went on to work in the field of computer security for a number of technology and computer companies. When Diffie heard that Martin Hellman, a professor at Stanford University in California, was working on the public-key problem, he promptly drove to California.

Martin Hellman (born in 1945) had grown up in a Jewish neighborhood of the Bronx, New York. He had a PhD in electrical engineering and had taught for several years at MIT before moving to Stanford. Hellman agreed to meet with Diffie, and the two hit it off. Hellman did not have enough funding to pay Diffie to work on his project, so Diffie enrolled in Stanford as a graduate student. They were eventually joined by computer scientist Ralph Merkle (born in 1952). Together they were able to develop the Diffie-Hellman-Merkle key-exchange method.

SOLVING THE PUBLIC-KEY PROBLEM

The solution to the key-exchange problem uses a special mathematical function (a formula to manipulate numbers) to allow the sender and receiver of a message to create a shared key known only to them. The mathematical function used to create the private key requires two numbers— one from the sender and one from the receiver—to generate the key: a third number known only to the two correspondents. The system relies on the sender and receiver to exchange this information

Alice

Bob

Common paint

+   +

Secret colours

=   =

Public transport

(assume that mixture separation is expensive)

+   +

Secret colours

=   =

Common secret

In a Diffie-Hellman-Merkle key-exchange example using two people, each party adds a secret color to a known color; each exchanges the mixed paint and adds a secret color to the bucket that each receives, creating the same color (the message).

JAMES ELLIS: TOP SECRET

James Ellis (1924–1997) and his group at the UK's Government Communications Headquarters (GCHQ) in Cheltenham, England, worked out a form of public-key cryptography in the 1970s, independently of Diffie, Hellman, and Merkle, but because the work was classified as top secret in the United Kingdom, this fact was not known until recently. Ellis grew up in the working-class area of London's East End, graduated from Imperial College, London, with a degree in physics, and started working for the GCHQ in Eastcote, West London, in 1952. In 1965, he moved to the new facility at Cheltenham as part of the new Communications-Electronics Security Group. In the late 1960s, the UK government was looking ahead to a time when miniaturization would allow all soldiers to have communications devices in the field, and the military began searching for a way for them to send and receive encrypted radio messages without having a secret key delivered to them. In 1969, the military asked Ellis to investigate the key-distribution problem. His solution to the problem, which he called nonsecret encryption, was similar to Diffie and Hellman's ideas, but he was forbidden to reveal anything about his top-secret work at the GCHQ, so nobody knew what he had discovered. After the publication of Diffie and Hellman's papers, the GCHQ released information about Ellis's contributions to public-key cryptography.

exclusively with each other. This process is known as the Diffie-Hellman-Merkle key exchange.

Diffie, Hellman, and Merkle demonstrated their process at the National Computer Conference in 1976 and patented it in 1977. The concept astounded their audience because for the first time two parties didn't have to meet to exchange a secret key.

Diffie and Hellman went a step further: they proposed the idea of a new form of cipher. Up to this point, all encryption/decryption processes had used the same key for both encryption and decryption. Diffie invented a way to use one key for encryption and a different key for decryption. In this scenario, a correspondent makes up two keys and publishes one of them—this is called the public key. Anyone who wants to send that person messages uses this key to encrypt them. This key cannot be used to decrypt the message, however. Instead, the correspondent has a second, private key, which he or she uses to decrypt the message. Diffie and Hellman published their concept in a paper titled "New Directions in Cryptography." Although they did not develop the mathematical solution to this method, their work initiated the search for the solution, which was ultimately supplied by Ronald Rivest, Adi Shamir, and Leonard Adleman of the Massachusetts Institute of Technology Laboratory for Computer Science.

In 2015, Diffie and Hellman were awarded the prestigious Turing Award by the Association for Computing Machinery for their groundbreaking work in public-key cryptography and digital signatures, "which are the foundation for most regularly-used security protocols on the Internet today."

GLOSSARY

advocate To encourage support for.

alliance An agreement between two nations to support each
other in military or political activities.

arbitrator An expert appointed by a court to resolve a dispute.

assassination Murder, usually for political reasons.

attaché An government representative.

besiege To surround a town or fortress with a military force so
that inhabitants cannot leave and supplies cannot be brought in.

brevet A military promotion given in return for outstanding
service.

combatant A person who fights in an armed conflict.

crib A word or phrase whose encryption pattern is known that is
given to a decoding device to allow it to start breaking a code.

decrypt To convert from coded form to readable text.

devastating Causing extreme distress.

dissident Someone who challenges the established rules.

dominance Mastery over.

encrypt To convert from readable text to a coded message.

espionage Spying.

extensive Covering a large area.

Huguenots A sect of French Protestants.

illicit Illegal.

incomprehensible Impossible to understand.

insurmountable Unable to be conquered.

military intelligence The acquisition and analysis of
information about enemy military activities.

Nationalist A member of a political group fighting for the independence of his or her country.

nonaggression pact An agreement among countries not to attack one another, often for a certain number of years.

polyalphabetic Using more than one alphabet.

purview Area of authority, control, or concern.

tract A short publication.

transpose To move a word from one place to another in a message.

FOR MORE INFORMATION

Canadian Security Intelligence Service (CSIS)
715 Rue Peel
Montréal, QC H3C 1B2
Canada
(514) 393-5600
Website: https://www.csis-scrs.gc.ca
The CSIS collects and analyzes intelligence information for the protection
of Canada and its people.

Central Intelligence Agency (CIA)
1000 Colonial Farm Road
McLean, VA 22101
(703) 482-0623
Website: https://www.cia.gov
The CIA collects foreign intelligence information to maintain US security.
It maintains a museum and offers a scholarship program for high
school seniors.

Communications Security Establishment (CSE)
1929 Ogilvie Road
Gloucester, ON K1G 3Z4
Canada
(613) 991-7248

Website: https://www.cse-cst.gc.ca
The CSE is the agency in Canada responsible for the collection of foreign
intelligence information required to keep the country secure.

Federal Bureau of Investigation (FBI)
935 Pennsylvania Avenue, NW
Washington, DC 20535-0001
(202) 324-3000
Website: https://www.fbi.gov
The FBI investigates criminal activities, including hacking, cybercrime,
and terrorism and collects intelligence information relating to these
activities. It also maintains the Crime Museum at its headquarters.

International Spy Museum
800 F Street NW
Washington, DC 20004
(202) 393-7798
Website: http://www.spymuseum.org
The International Spy Museum offers an extensive collection
of artifacts and special exhibits on the history, craft, and
influence of espionage.

National Cryptological Museum
National Security Agency
Fort Meade, MD 20755
(301) 688-5849
Website: https://www.nsa.gov/about/
cryptologic_heritage/museum

Located adjacent to NSA headquarters at Fort Meade, Maryland, the National Cryptological Museum houses artifacts related to the history of the cryptologic field as well as special exhibits and library.

WEBSITES

Because of the changing nature of internet links, Rosen Publishing has developed an online list of websites related to the subject of this book. This site is updated regularly. Please use this link to access the list:

http://www.rosenlinks.com/CCMCB/famous

FOR FURTHER READING

Bauer, Craig P. *Secret History: The Story of Cryptology*. Boca Raton, FL: CRC Press, 2013.

Copeland, B. Jack. *Colossus: The Secrets of Bletchley Park's Code-Breaking Computers*. New York, NY: Oxford University Press, 2010.

D'Agapeyeff, Alexander. *Codes and Ciphers: A History of Cryptography*. N.p.: Hesperides Press, 2008.

Donovan, Peter, and John Mack. *Code Breaking in the Pacific*. New York, NY: Springer, 2014.

Dooley, John F. *Codes, Ciphers, and Spies: Tales of Military Intelligence in World War I*. New York, NY: Springer, 2016.

Gregory, Jillian. *Breaking Secret Codes*. North Mankato, MN: Capstone Press, 2011.

Gregory, Jillian. *Making Secret Codes*. North Mankato, MN: Capstone Press, 2011.

Hastings, Max. *The Secret War: Spies, Ciphers, and Guerillas, 1939–1945*. New York, NY: HarperCollins, 2016.

Johnson, Bud. *Break the Code: Cryptography for Beginners*. Mineola, NY: Dover Publications, 1997.

Maffeo, Steven E. *U.S. Navy Codebreakers, Linguists, and Intelligence Officers Against Japan, 1910–1941*. Lanham, MD: Rowan & Littlefield, 2016.

McKay, Sinclair. *The Secret Lives of Codebreakers: The Men and Women Who Cracked the Enigma Code at Bletchley Park*. New York, NY: Plume, 2012.

Nez, Chester, and Judith Scheiss Avila. *Code Talker: The First and Only Memoir by One of the Original Navajo Code Talkers of World War II*. Audiobook. Old Saybrook, CT: Tantor Media, 2011.

Nickels, Hamilton. *Secrets of Making and Breaking Codes: A Hands-on Guide to Both Simple and Sophisticated Codes to Easily Help You Become a Codemaster*. New York, NY: Skyhorse Publishing, 2014.

Sutherland, Denise, and Mark E. Kolto-Rivera. *Cracking Codes and Cryptograms for Dummies*. Hoboken, NJ: John Wiley and Sons, 2010.

Yardley, Herbert O. *The American Black Chamber*. Ebook. Annapolis, MD: Naval Institute Press, 2013.

BIBLIOGRAPHY

Association for Computing Machinery. "A. M. Turing Award: Whitfield Diffie." Retrieved May 30, 2016. http://amturing.acm.org/award_winners/diffie_8371646.cfm.

BBC. "History: Bletchley Park." Retrieved March 27, 2016. http://www.bbc.co.uk/history/places/bletchley_park.

Davies, Carolyn. "PM's Apology to Codebreaker Alan Turing: We Were Inhumane." *The Guardian*, September 10, 2009.

Encyclopedia Britannica. "Polybius." Retrieved February 29, 2016. http://www.britannica.com/biography/Polybius.

Federal Communications Commission. "A Short History of Radio." Retrieved March 21, 2016. https://transition.fcc.gov/omd/history/radio/documents/short_history.pdf.

Ford, Brian J. *Secret Weapons: Technology, Science & the Race to Win World War II*. Long Island City, NY: Osprey Publishing Company, 2011.

Gaddy, David W. "Internal Struggle: The Civil War." Retrieved March 19, 2016. http://www.civilwarsignals.org/pages/crypto/crypto.html.

Hagen, Carey. "The Coast Guard's Most Potent Weapon during Prohibition? Elizabeth Friedman." Smithsonian.com. Retrieved March 21, 2016. http://www.smithsonianmag.com/history/coast-guards-most-potent-weapon-during-prohibition-codebreaker-elizebeth-friedman-180954066/?no-ist.

Livius. "Polybius." Retrieved February 29, 2016. http://www.livius.org/articles/person/polybius.

National Security Agency. "Madame X: Agnes Mary Driscoll and Naval Cryptology 1919–1940." Cryptographic Almanac 50th Anniversary

Series. Retrieved March 21, 2016. https://www.nsa.gov/public_info /_files/crypto_almanac_50th/madame_x_agnes_meyer_driscoll.pdf

National Security Agency. "The Many Lives of Herbert O. Yardley." Retrieved March 27, 2016. https://www.nsa.gov/public_info/_files /cryptologic_spectrum/many_lives.pdf.

National Security Agency Center for Cryptologic History. "Masked Dispatches: Cryptograms and Cryptology in American History." Meade, MD: NSA, 2013.

Northern Kentucky University. "Desiderata for Military Cryptography." Retrieved March 19, 2016. http://www.nku.edu/~christensen /092hnr304%20kerckhoffs%20principles.pdf.

Pincock, Stephen. *Codebreaker: The History of Codes and Ciphers, from the Ancient Pharaohs to Quantum Cryptography*. New York, NY: Walker, 2006.

Singh, Simon. *The Code Book: The Science of Secrecy from Ancient Egypt to Quantum Cryptography*. New York, NY: Random House, 2000.

Wilcox, Jennifer. "Sharing the Burden: Women in Cryptology During World War II." Mead, MD: National Security Agency Center for Cryptologic History, 2013.

INDEX

ABOUT THE AUTHOR

Jeri Freedman has a BA from Harvard University. For fifteen years, she worked in the high-technology field. She is the author of more than fifty young adult nonfiction books, including *Great Debates: Civil Liberties and Terrorism*, *Great Debates: Privacy vs. Security*, *Careers in Security*, and *Tech in the Trenches: World War II*.

PHOTO CREDITS

Cover, p. 3 (background) Mclek/Shutterstock.com; cover, p. 3 (Diffie), p. 48 Gabriel Bouys/AFP/Getty Images; p. 7 MPI/Archive Photos/Getty Images; p. 11 Private Collection/Bridgeman Images; pp. 13, 14 SPL/Science Source; p. 16 akg-images /Newscom; p. 17 Middle Temple Library/Science Source; p. 19 Encyclopaedia Britannica/Universal Images Group/Getty Images; p. 21 Le traite des chiffres /Bridgeman Images; p. 23 Library of Congress Prints and Photographs Division; pp. 24, 43 Science & Society Picture Library/Getty Images; p. 25 Used by permission. Special Collections, Jasper County Public Library; pp. 30, 47 Private Collection/Prismatic Pictures/Bridgeman Images; p. 32 National Cryptologic Museum, David Kahn Collection; pp. 34, 39 Courtesy of the George C. Marshall Foundation, Lexington, Virginia; p. 37 Bettmann/Getty Images; p. 44 PhotoQuest/Archive Photos/Getty Images; p. 46 neftali/Shutterstock.com; p. 50 Wikimedia Commons / File:Diffie-Hellman Key Exchange.svg; back cover and interior pages (binary numbers pattern) © iStockphoto.com/Vjom; interior pages (numbers and letters pattern) © iStockphoto.com/maxkabakov.

Designer: Matt Cauli; Senior Editor: Kathy Kuhtz Campbell; Photo Researcher: Bruce Donnola